American VOICES

BY JOHN JACOBSON AND ROGER EMERSON

Celebrating America from Armistice to the Moon

TABLE OF CONTENTS

MUSICAL PERFORMANCE RIGHTS

HAL•LEONARD®
CORPORATION
7777 W. BLUEMOUND RD. P.O. BOX 13819 MILWAUKEE, WI 53213

Visit Hal Leonard Online at
www.halleonard.com

1. AMERICAN VOICES

Words and Music by JOHN JACOBSON
and ROGER EMERSON

sing - ing one A - mer - i - can song!

A - mer - i - can voic - es

sing - ing one A - mer - i - can song;_____

sing - ing one A -

rit.

mer - i - can song!_____

SCENE 1

Theodore Roosevelt: *(dressed like a Rough Rider)* "I think there is only one quality worse than hardness of heart and that is softness of head."

Speaker 1: That's president Theodore Roosevelt, the 26th President of the United States and one of the most colorful voices of America.

T. Roosevelt: "Believe you can and you're halfway there!"

Speaker 2: Before Theodore Roosevelt was president, he was a member of the 1st United States Volunteer Academy, known forever as the Rough Riders, for indeed they were!

Speaker 3: A determined conservationist and a true patriot, Roosevelt became president at the start of a brand new century in the young nation called the United States of America.

T. Roosevelt: "Do what you can, with what you have, where you are."

Speaker 4: By the time America was only one hundred years old, it had already made its mark as one of the greatest nations in the history of civilization.

Speaker 5: Yet, we had only eight thousand cars and ten miles of paved roads.

Speaker 6: The average worker made $12.98 … *(pause)* … a week!

Speaker 7: President Roosevelt said …

T. Roosevelt: "The government is us; **we** are the government, you and I."

Speaker 7: Then he said,

T. Roosevelt: "Far and away, the best prize life has to offer is the chance to work hard at work worth doing."

Speaker 7: And finally he said,

T. Roosevelt: "I am only an average man but, by George, I work harder at it than the average man!"

Speaker 8: That was the character of 1901 America.

Speaker 9: As the world turned into a new century, America was turning into a place where everybody wanted to be!

Speaker 10: *(excitedly)* Patriotism reached new highs in 1904 and the place to be was Saint Louis, Missouri for the Louisiana Purchase Exposition, more commonly known as The World's Fair!

SONG 2: AMERICANA MEDLEY

2. AMERICANA MEDLEY

Words and Music by JOHN JACOBSON
and ROGER EMERSON

MEET ME IN ST. LOUIS, LOUIS
Words by Andrew B. Sterling
Music by Kerry Mills

* pronounced: *loo-ee*

BILL BAILEY, WON'T YOU PLEASE COME HOME
Words and Music by Hughie Cannon

March (♩ = 120)

YOU'RE A GRAND OLD FLAG
Words and Music by George M. Cohan

You're a grand old flag, you're a high fly - ing flag; and for - ev - er in peace may you wave.

You're the em - blem of the land I love. The home of the free and the brave.

Ev - 'ry heart beats true un - der red, white and blue, where there's nev - er a boast or brag.

But should auld ac - quain - tance be for -

(melody in lower notes)

got, keep your eye on the grand

old flag!

SCENE 2

(Add dialogue to Scene 2 Underscore – Scott Joplin's "The Entertainer")

Speaker 11: The year is 1918, at the eleventh hour of the eleventh day of the eleventh month.

Newspaper Hawker: "Extra Extra! Read all about it! The war to end all wars is over!"

Speaker 12: The country and the world were emerging from a rough era of war and epidemic. There was even talk of revenge against the countries that seemed to have caused the conflict.

Speaker 13: But President Woodrow Wilson said …

Woodrow Wilson: "Peace has to be a peace of reconciliation, a peace without victory, for a victor's peace would leave a sting, a resentment, a bitter memory upon which terms of peace would rest, not permanently, but only as upon quicksand."

Speaker 14: From this idea, the League of Nations was born. President Wilson said this about America …

Woodrow Wilson: "America is not anything if it consists of each of us. It is something only if it consists of **all** of us."

Speaker 15: All together, America was ready to celebrate and have some fun! So the 1920s came in with a roar and a dance that was the cat's meow!

WON'T YOU COME DO THE CHARLESTON

Words and Music by ROGER EMERSON
and RICHARD DERWINGSON

Won't you____ come do____ the Charles-ton?____

Strike up the band! Give 'em____ a hand! Sing out the news!

Won't you____ come do____ the Charles-ton?___

Join in thesong. Come on____ a-long. It's up to you.

Danc-in', danc-in', don't be shy.____ Danc-in',

glanc-in' eye to eye,_ my, oh my!_

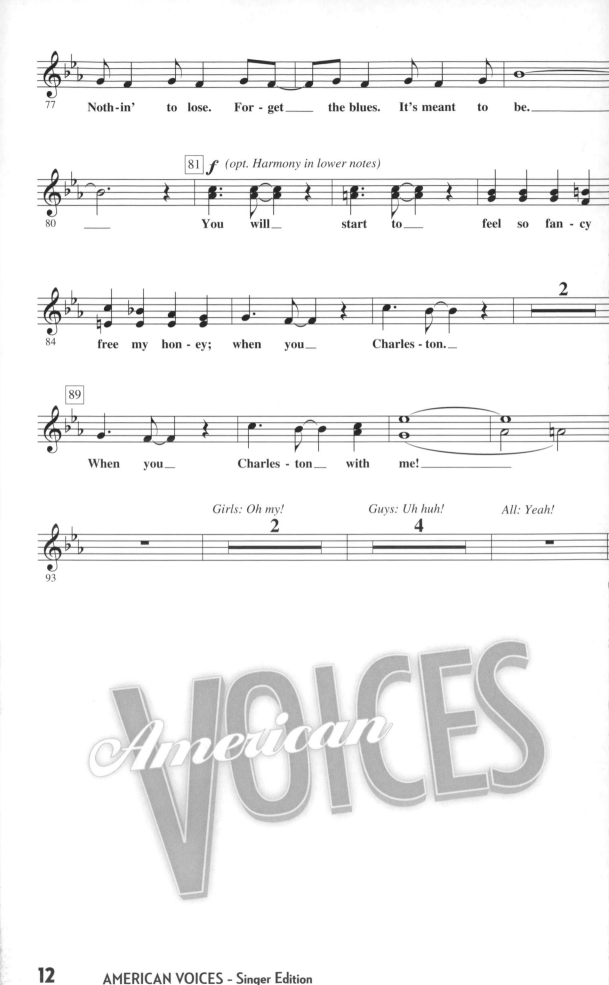

Noth-in' to lose. For - get ___ the blues. It's meant to be. ___

81 *f (opt. Harmony in lower notes)*

___ You will ___ start to ___ feel so fan - cy

free my hon - ey; when you ___ Charles - ton. ___

89

When you ___ Charles - ton ___ with me! ___

Girls: Oh my! *Guys: Uh huh!* *All: Yeah!*

SCENE 3

Newspaper Hawker: Extra! Extra! Read all about it. October 29, 1929—Black Tuesday! Wall Street Crashes! Great Depression begins.

Speaker 16: For the next 12 years, America and the rest of the western industrialized world suffered what has come to be known as the Great Depression. The Dust Bowl, bank closures, a collapse in agriculture and other problems plagued the nation and times were hard.

Speaker 17: America bent, but it did not break. President Franklin Roosevelt said …

FDR: "I pledge you, I pledge myself, to a new deal for the American People!"

Speaker 18: Not everybody loved President Roosevelt's New Deal, but there was definitely a new feeling in the 1930s.

Speaker 19: America rolled up its sleeves and got to work, finding happiness and satisfaction in the joy of upbeat song and dance!

SONG 4: THE NEW DEAL JUMP

4. THE NEW DEAL JUMP

Words and Music by JOHN JACOBSON
and ROGER EMERSON

Ev - 'ry - bod - y jump.
Can you take the heat?

new deal!

21 *All: both times*

Ev - 'ry - one is do - in' it. Things are look - in' up. Got a

dol - lar in my pock - et, two bits in my cup. It's a new deal!

1 Group I

It's a new deal! It's a

2 **30**

Jump, jump, jump! Ev - 'ry - bod - y

jump, jump, jump! Ev - 'ry - bod - y jump, jump,

jump! Ev - 'ry - bod - y jump, jump, jump! Ev - 'ry - bod - y

(opt. Harmony in lower notes)

2

jump! Do - in' the new deal jump!

Instrumental DANCE BREAK "The New Deal Jump"
(2nd time: Sing over instruments on repeat)

Jump, jump, jump. Ev - 'ry - bod - y jump, jump,

jump. Ev - 'ry - bod - y jump, jump, jump. Ev - 'ry - bod - y

jump, jump, jump. Ev - 'ry - bod - y jump.

Do - in' the new deal jump!

Ev - 'ry - bod - y jump. Do - in' the new deal...

jump!_____ Jump, jump, jump, jump, jump!

SCENE 4

Speaker 20: World War I was supposed to be the war to end all wars, but that was not the case.

Speaker 21: In the 1940s, World War II broke out, and American soldiers were back in the battlefields of Europe and Asia.

Speaker 22: Young women were working in factories at home to support the war and as nurses on the warfront.

Speaker 23: Young men were signing up in droves and being shipped all over the world as defenders of freedom and liberty.

Speaker 24: Once again, families and friends were separated and the loneliness of war took a toll on all Americans.

Speaker 25: Yet, it was a promise of being back together with family and friends that helped boyfriends and girlfriends, brothers and sisters, moms and dads and all fellow Americans survive the pain of separation and believe in brighter days ahead.

(On one side of the stage is a soldier writing a letter. He reads aloud as he writes. Mom and Dad sit on the other side of the stage, reading the letter.)

Soldier: "Dear Mom and Pop,

It has been almost eleven months since I last saw you, but I look at your picture many times a day and night, and read your letters over and over. This war in Europe rages on and on, as it does in Asia and it seems like every other part of the world.

Soldier and Mom: I cannot tell you where I am … *(soldier fades out)*

Mom: *(continues reading)* … but it is cold and wet and lonely as can be. I can't wait until this war is over and I can come home. No need to worry, Mom and Pop, I'll be home real soon."

SONG 5: I'LL BE HOME REAL SOON
(Soldier continues writing.)

5. I'LL BE HOME REAL SOON

Words and Music by JOHN JACOBSON
and ROGER EMERSON

Lyrics:

The days are lone-ly, the nights are long,_ as I sit writ-ing my sad, sad song._

I prom-ise you, as I gaze at the moon___ that I'll be home,_ I'll be home real soon.

So far from home, I'm so sad and blue._ I on-ly smile when I think of you._

When we're a-part my song is out of tune.___ But I'll be home,_ I'll be home real soon.

that I'll be home, ___ I'll be home real soon.

I'll be home real soon. I'll be home real soon.

I'll be home real soon. _____

SCENE 5

Speaker 26: At last, the long war was over in Europe and in Asia. The men ...

Girl Speaker: And women …

Speaker 26: Were coming home!

Speaker 27: Ironically, the war was actually a boost to the American economy and hope for happy and brighter days ahead made America a happy and "happening" place to be!

Big Bopper: Hello, Baaaaaby! Welcome to 1959! Things are looking up, boys and girls! World War II is over! The economy is pumping along. America is feeling good. So get your poodle skirts, slick back your hair, get your daddy's T-Bird 'cause America's on a rock and roll!!

SONG 6: WE'RE ON A ROCK AND ROLL

6. WE'RE ON A ROCK AND ROLL

Words and Music by JOHN JACOBSON
and ROGER EMERSON

25 Get up off your chair. Slick back your hair.

27 Come a - long and rock with me!____

32

30 ____ Ev - 'ry - bod - y Fred - dy.

33 Fred - dy if you're read - y, on - ly with your

36 stead - y. We're on a rock and roll!____

40

39 Ev - 'ry - bod - y rock. Ev - 'ry - bod - y

42 roll. Things__ are look - in' up.

45 We're on a rock and roll!____

48 DANCE BREAK

12

SCENE 6

Eleanor Roosevelt: "The future belongs to those who believe in the beauty of their dreams."

Speaker 28: That's Eleanor Roosevelt – First Lady of the United States from 1933 to 1945.

Speaker 29: Even after her years in the White House, Mrs. Roosevelt continued to be one of the most influential women in American History.

Speaker 30: She was a champion for civil rights, the new idea of the United Nations and, of course, women's rights.

Eleanor Roosevelt: "A woman is like a tea bag. You can't tell how strong she is until you put her in hot water!"

John Kennedy: "And so, my fellow Americans, ask not what your country can do for you; ask what you can do for your country."

Speaker 31: World War II hero John Kennedy became president of the United States in 1960 and challenged America to set lofty goals for its future.

John Kennedy: "As we set sail, we ask God's blessing on the most hazardous and dangerous and greatest adventure on which man has ever embarked!"

Speaker 32: VERY lofty.

John Kennedy: "We choose to go to the moon."

Speaker 32: See what I mean?

John Kennedy: "We choose to go to the moon and do these other things, not because they are easy ... but because they are hard."

Speaker 33: This was the spirit of America in the 1950s and '60s, and the idea of a great, young nation burned ever brighter.

John Kennedy: "A man may die, nations may rise and fall, but an idea lives on."

Speaker 34: Our best ideas have always been the ones we worked on together as a nation to bring to reality.

John Kennedy:	"In a very real sense, it will not be one man going to the moon, it will be an entire nation. For all of us must work to put him there."
Speaker 35:	The common dream of a great nation was being passed from one generation to the next.
John Kennedy:	"Let the word go forth from this time and place, to friend and foe alike, that the torch has been passed to a new generation of Americans …"

SONG 7: THIS LITTLE LIGHT OF MINE
(Underscore choir humming "We Shall Overcome")

Eleanor Roosevelt:	*(repeating herself, very sincerely)* "The future belongs to those who believe in the beauty of their dreams."
Martin Luther King, Jr.:	"I still have a dream. It is a dream deeply rooted in the American Dream."
Speaker 36:	That's Doctor Martin Luther King, Jr. speaking of the hope of the American Dream.
MLK:	"I have a dream that my children will one day live in a nation where they will not be judged by the color of their skin, but by the content of their character."
Speaker 37:	The 1960s and '70s were important growing up years in this great country called America. In some ways, they were difficult years indeed.
Speaker 38:	But for those that believe in the beauty of the dream, we also believe that after each struggle, America comes out better on the other side.
Eleanor Roosevelt:	"It is better to light a candle than curse the darkness."
Speaker 39:	That's the real dream of all of America's true Voices!

(continue song, singing "This Little Light of Mine")

7. THIS LITTLE LIGHT OF MINE
(with "We Shall Overcome")

Traditional
Arranged by ROGER EMERSON

(Speaker 39: That's the real dream of all of America's true voices!)

SCENE 7

(Use music to underscore this dialogue or as scene change music after the dialogue.)

Hippy 1: Hey, man! Can you tell me how to get to Woodstock?

Uptight Adult 1: *(about to faint)* Oh dear! Honey! I believe that man is a ... a ... hippy!

Uptight Adult 2: I can't tell if it's a boy or a girl with that long hair.

Uptight Adult 1: Be careful, dear. You don't know what they've been into.

Hippy 2: You gotta chill, man. We're just happy to be alive.

Speaker 40: It's so true. In the 1960s and '70s, there were a lot of Americans disillusioned by yet another war and what seemed to be an impossible generation gap.

Speaker 41: Many were tired of wars overseas and cultural wars at home.

Speaker 42: America was ready for a period of peace, love and brotherhood.

Hippy 1: Right on!

8. PEACE, LOVE AND BROTHERHOOD

Words and Music by JOHN JACOBSON
and ROGER EMERSON

Peace, love and broth - er - hood,_ walk - ing hand in_ hand._

(opt. Harmony in lower notes)

Peace, love and sis - ter - hood, a - cross this great big_ land._

All we are ask - ing for is love._

All we are seek - ing_ is peace.

All we are ask - ing for is hap - pi - ness;_ for war and strife to_ cease.

39
Peace,   love   and   broth - er - hood, __

43
walk - ing   hand   in __ hand. __

47
Peace,   love   and   sis - ter - hood,   a - cross   this

2
52
great   big __ land. _____

57
We   can   build   a   world   full   of   love. _____

61
We   can   build   a   world   of __ peace.

65
We   can   build   a   world   full   of   hap - pi - ness; __ where

69
war   and   strife   will __ cease.

SCENE 8

(Add dialogue to Scene 8 Underscore)

Speaker 43: Listen! American Voices!

Speaker 44: Eleanor Roosevelt said: "You gain strength, courage, and confidence by every experience in which you really stop to look fear in the face."

Speaker 45: Woodrow Wilson said, "America lives in the heart of every man who wishes to find a region where he will be free to work out his destiny as he chooses."

Speaker 46: Theodore Roosevelt said, "This country will not be a good place for any of us to live in, unless we make it a good place for **all** of us to live in."

Speaker 47: As he stepped onto the moon surface, Neil Armstrong said, "This is one small step for man; one giant leap for mankind."

Speaker 48: And America indeed did take giant steps forward.

Speaker 49: Today there is a new set of voices in this great land called America!

Speaker 50: WE…who stand before you now, are the new American Voices.

Speaker 51: As we grow and learn from those who have gone before us, we add our own voices to the chorus that make up the beauty of the American Song.

Speaker 52: I pledge allegiance . . .

(As Speaker 52 continues to recite the Pledge, another few speakers start reciting the Pledge from the beginning – each at their own pace; when they get to the word "allegiance," add more speakers, and so on. As each speaker gets to the end of the Pledge, they start over again. It should sound like a cacophony of sound with all voicesoverlapping at different parts of the pledge. When last voice starts the pledge, all voices come together and say the entire Pledge together in unison. See Production Guide pg. 6 for more direction.)

All: *(last time, with all voices in unison)*

"I pledge allegiance to the flag
of the United States of America,
and to the Republic for which it stands,

(getting louder) one nation, under God, indivisible

(music cuts out) with liberty and justice for all!"

9. REPRISE: AMERICAN VOICES
(with "America, the Beautiful")

Arranged by JOHN JACOBSON
and ROGER EMERSON

CODA

A - mer - i - can voic-

es   sing-ing   ev - 'ry - where.

opt. Harmony

Ah

Ah

A - mer - i - can voic   -   es   e - cho   in   the   air.

Ah

A - mer - i - can voic   -   es

Ah

proud   and   clear   and   strong.   A - mer - i - can voic-

Ah

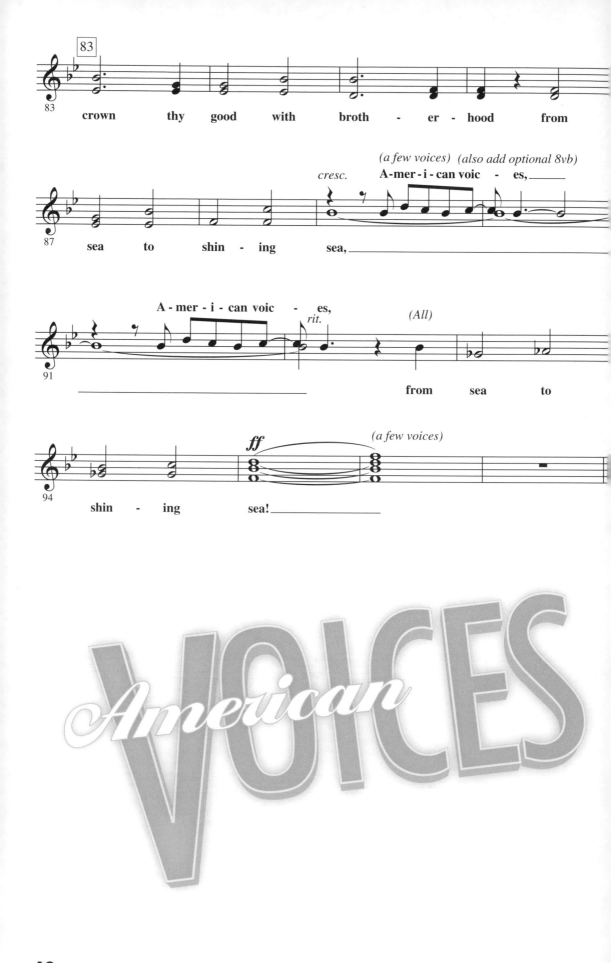